God Restores

Prayers & Promises for Restoration

By Violet James, MSM

MP
Maximum Potential, LLC

Table of Contents

INTRODUCTION

Though you have made me see troubles, many and bitter, you will restore my life again; from the depths of the earth you will again bring me up. (Psalm 71:20, NIV)

If you need restoration in any area of your life, God promises that He will comfort you, heal your pain and sorrow, strengthen you and lift you back up. *"He restores my soul; He leads me in the paths of righteousness for His name's sake" (Psalm 23:3, NKJV). "The LORD is close to the brokenhearted and saves those who are crushed in spirit" (Psalm 34:18, NIV).*

Throughout the Bible, we see that God restores. He is our Restorer. According to Webster's dictionary, the definition of restore is to give back, return, reestablish to a former, more desirable condition; to bring back to a state of health, soundness, or vigor; to put back, return, as to a former place, position, or rank. And, not only does God restore but He restores it better than it was before. We see this in Job 42:10, "And the LORD restored Job's losses when he prayed for his friends. Indeed the LORD gave Job twice as much as he had before." God can restore any area in your life.

Sometimes we need restoration because of our own mistakes, bad choices, sin, etc. But other times, we experience injustices against us or pain/loss and tragedy that we had no control over. As a result, we may experience intense pain, anger, unforgiveness, frustration, regret, feelings of rejection from people and God, confusion, sadness, and other intense emotions. In the midst of our pain, God will never leave us or forsake us. He is holding us in His loving arms, surrounding us with His love, comfort and peace that passes all understanding. God promises that He will be close to us, heal our pain and suffering, and reestablish and renew our lives. We can have peace, strength and joy again.

This book contains specific prayers for restoration with related Scriptures to meditate on. Remember that God's mercies are new every morning. It is my prayer that, "the God of all grace, who called you to his eternal glory in Christ, after you have suffered a little while, will himself restore you and make you strong, firm and steadfast" *(1 Peter 5:10, NIV)*.

God bless, Violet

"So I will restore to you the years that the swarming locust has eaten..." (Joel 2:25a, NKJV)

"He heals the brokenhearted and binds up their wounds." (Psalm 147:3, NKJV)

"Return to your fortress, you prisoners of hope; even now I announce that I will restore twice as much to you." (Zechariah 9:12; NIV)

"I will make rivers flow on the dry hills
and springs flow through the valleys.
I will change the desert into a lake of water
and the dry land into fountains of water.
I will make trees grow in the desert—
cedars, acacia, myrtle, and olive trees.
I will put pine, fir, and cypress trees
growing together in the desert.
People will see these things and understand;
they will think carefully about these things and
learn that the LORD's power did this,
that the Holy One of Israel made these things."
(Isaiah 41:18-20, NCV)

"Finally, brothers and sisters, rejoice! Strive for full restoration, encourage one another, be of one mind, live in peace. And the God of love and peace will be with you." (2 Corinthians 13:11, NIV)

God Restores My Peace

Personal Prayer:

Dear Heavenly Father,

I am coming to You, weary, troubled and heavy burdened and You promise to give me rest for my soul. I am struggling to experience your peace. Worry, doubts, fears, uncertainties, and unexpected circumstances are robbing me of inner peace. Lord, help me to keep my mind on You and place my trust in You alone. I give all my worries and cares to You for You care and love me deeply. Even in the midst of difficult times, You give me inner peace that passes all understanding and guards my heart and mind. When I lie down, I will not be afraid and my sleep will be sweet. Thank you for restoring my peace, giving me rest, and refreshing my soul.

Scriptures to Meditate On:

Give your burdens to the LORD, and he will take care of you. He will not permit the godly to slip and fall. *(Psalm 55:22, NLT)*

Give all your worries and cares to God, for he cares about you. *(1 Peter 5:7, NLT)*

And the peace of God, which transcends all understanding, will guard your hearts and your minds in Christ Jesus. *(Philippians 4:7, NIV)*

"Come to me, all you who are weary and burdened, and I will give you rest. Take my yoke upon you and learn from me, for I am gentle and humble in heart, and you will find rest for your souls. For my yoke is easy and my burden is light." *(Matthew 11:28-30, NIV)*

Peace I leave with you; my peace I give you. I do not give to you as the world gives. Do not let your hearts be troubled and do not be afraid. *(John 14:27, NIV)*

"I have told you these things, so that in me you may have peace. In this world you will have trouble. But take heart! I have overcome the world." *(John 16:33, NIV)*

You will keep him in perfect peace, whose mind is stayed on You, because he trusts in You. *(Isaiah 26:3, NKJV)*

When you lie down, you will not be afraid; Yes, you will lie down and your sleep will be sweet. *(Proverbs 3:24, NKJV)*

The LORD is my shepherd, I lack nothing. He makes me lie down in green pastures, He leads me beside quiet waters, He refreshes my soul. He guides me along the right paths for his name's sake. *(Psalm 23:1-3)*

God Restores My Hope

Personal Prayer:

Dear Heavenly Father,

I am completely discouraged and my heart is sad. Revive me by your Word. Let your unfailing love surround me, Lord, for my hope is in You alone. When doubts fill my mind, your comfort and peace give me renewed hope and cheer. Lead me by your truth and teach me, for you are the God who saves me. All day long I put my hope in you. You said in your Word that You have good plans for me, plans to prosper me and not to harm me, plans to give me hope and a future. I will put my trust and hope in You. I will praise you, my Savior and my God. May You, the God of hope, fill me with all joy and peace as I trust in You, so that I may overflow with hope by the power of the Holy Spirit.

Scriptures to Meditate On:

I am completely discouraged—I lie in the dust. Revive me by your Word. *(Psalm 119:25, TLB)*

Why am I discouraged?
  Why is my heart so sad?
I will put my hope in God!
  I will praise him again—
  my Savior and my God! *(Psalm 43:5, NLT)*

3

When doubts filled my mind, your comfort gave me renewed hope and cheer. *(Psalm 94:19, NLT)*

May the God of hope fill you with all joy and peace as you trust in him, so that you may overflow with hope by the power of the Holy Spirit. *(Romans 15:13, NIV)*

"For I know the plans I have for you," declares the LORD, "plans to prosper you and not to harm you, plans to give you hope and a future." *(Jeremiah 29:11, NIV)*

This I recall to my mind,
Therefore I have hope.
Through the LORD's mercies we are not consumed,
because His compassions fail not.
They are new every morning;
Great is Your faithfulness.
"The LORD is my portion," says my soul,
"Therefore I hope in Him!"
The LORD is good to those who wait for Him,
To the soul who seeks Him.
It is good that one should hope and wait quietly
For the salvation of the LORD.
(Lamentations 3:21-26, NKJV)

Lead me by your truth and teach me, for you are the God who saves me. All day long I put my hope in you. *(Psalm 25:5, NLT)*

Let your unfailing love surround us, Lord, for our hope is in you alone. *(Psalm 33:22, NKJV)*

4

And so, Lord, where do I put my hope? My only hope is in you. *(Psalm 39:7, NLT)*

I wait for the LORD, my soul waits, And in His word I do hope. *(Psalm 130:5, NKJV)*

Recommended Resources:

Finding Hope in God *by Krystal Kuehn*

Depression: Breaking Free From its Grip *by Krystal Kuehn*

God Restores My Dreams

Personal Prayer:

Dear Heavenly Father,

You created me for a specific purpose. I am Your masterpiece. You have plans to prosper me and to give me hope and a future. It is my heart's desire to accomplish what you created me to do. You know what would satisfy the deepest longings of my heart. And if I take delight in You, You will give me the desires of my heart. Even when adversity comes against me and keeps me from fulfilling my dreams and desires, You promise that my gifts and calling will never be withdrawn. Help me to trust in You with all my heart and not lean on my own understanding. As I seek Your will for my life, You promise to teach, guide and instruct me in which path and direction to take. Thank you, God. You restore my dreams and satisfy the desires of my heart.

Scriptures to Meditate On:

For we are God's masterpiece. He has created us anew in Christ Jesus, so we can do the good things he planned for us long ago. *(Ephesians 2:10, NLT)*

"For I know the plans I have for you," declares the Lord, "plans to prosper you and not to harm you, plans to give you hope and a future." *(Jeremiah 29:11, NIV)*

Take delight in the LORD, and he will give you the desires of your heart. *(Psalm 37:4, NIV)*

The LORD is near to all who call on him, to all who call on him in truth. He fulfills the desires of those who fear him; he hears their cry and saves them. *(Psalm 145: 18-19, NIV)*

For God's gifts and his call can never be withdrawn. *(Romans 11:29, NLT)*

Trust in the LORD with all your heart; do not depend on your own understanding. Seek his will in all you do, and he will show you which path to take. *(Proverbs 3:5-6, NLT)*

I will instruct you and teach you in the way you should go; I will guide you with My eye. *(Psalm 32:8)*

A man's heart plans his way, but the LORD directs his steps. *(Proverbs 16:9, NKJV)*

Do not conform to the pattern of this world, but be transformed by the renewing of your mind. Then you will be able to test and approve what God's will is— his good, pleasing and perfect will. *(Romans 12:2, NIV)*

God Restores My Strength

Personal Prayer:

Dear Heavenly Father,

My soul melts from heaviness. I feel faint and weary. My strength is gone and I can hardly breathe. Strengthen me according to Your word. For You are my refuge and strength, an ever-present help in trouble. I will wait on You and renew my strength. I will mount up with wings like eagles; I will run and not be weary; and I will walk and not faint. I will be strong in You and in Your mighty power. I will not be afraid or be discouraged, for You are with me wherever I go. I will not be dejected and sad, for the joy of the Lord is my strength. For it is You, Lord, who arms me with strength and keeps my way secure. You are the rock of my strength and my refuge is in You.

Scriptures to Meditate On:

Have I not commanded you? Be strong and courageous. Do not be afraid; do not be discouraged, for the LORD your God will be with you wherever you go. *(Joshua 1:9, NIV)*

Don't be dejected and sad, for the joy of the LORD is your strength! *(Nehemiah 8:10b, NLT)*

Even the youths shall faint and be weary,
And the young men shall utterly fall,
But those who wait on the LORD
Shall renew their strength;
They shall mount up with wings like eagles,
They shall run and not be weary,
They shall walk and not faint. *(Isaiah 40:30-31, NKJV)*

For the eyes of the LORD range throughout the earth to strengthen those whose hearts are fully committed to him. *(Chronicles 16:9a, NIV)*

Be of good courage,
And He shall strengthen your heart,
All you who hope in the LORD. *(Psalm 31:24, NKJV)*

It is God who arms me with strength and keeps my way secure. *(Psalm 18:32, NIV)*

The Lord is my strength and my shield; My heart trusted in Him, and I am helped; Therefore my heart greatly rejoices, And with my song I will praise Him. *(Psalm 28:7, NKJV)*

God is our refuge and strength, an ever-present help in trouble. *(Psalm 46:1, NIV)*

In God is my salvation and my glory; The rock of my strength, And my refuge, is in God. *(Psalm 62:7, NKJV)*

But the Lord is faithful, and he will strengthen you and protect you from the evil one. *(2 Thessalonians 3:3, NIV)*

God Restores My Health

Personal Prayer:

Dear Heavenly Father,

I will praise You, for I am fearfully and wonderfully made. You made my body and have the power to heal and restore it. It is Your will for me to be healthy and whole. I am redeemed from the curse of sickness. The blood that Jesus shed on the cross for my redemption was also shed that I might be free from sickness and disease for by His stripes I am healed. Your word is life to those who find it and health to one's whole body. Search me, God, and know my heart. If there is any offense or unforgiveness in me, help me to release it. Help my heart to be filled with peace, for a heart filled with peace gives life to the body. Thank You, Lord, for rising up with healing in Your wings. You are restoring my body and making me healthy and whole that I may fulfill the number of my days in health.

Scriptures to Meditate On:

I will praise You, for I am fearfully and wonderfully made; Marvelous are Your works, and that my soul knows very well. *(Psalm 139:14, NKJV)*

My son, pay attention to what I say; turn your ear to

my words. Do not let them out of your sight; keep them within your heart; for they are life to those who find them and health to one's whole body. *(Proverbs 4:20-22, NIV)*

Do not be wise in your own eyes; fear the LORD and depart from evil. It will be health to your flesh, and strength to your bones. *(Proverbs 3:7-8, NKJV)*

He sent out his word and healed them; he rescued them from the grave. *(Psalm 107:20, NIV)*

A man with leprosy came and knelt before him and said, "Lord, if you are willing, you can make me clean." Jesus reached out his hand and touched the man. "I am willing," he said. "Be clean!" Immediately he was cleansed of his leprosy. *(Matthew 8:2-3, NIV)*

But Christ has rescued us from the curse pronounced by the law. When he was hung on the cross, he took upon himself the curse for our wrongdoing. For it is written in the Scriptures, "Cursed is everyone who is hung on a tree." *(Galatians 3:13, NLT)*

Surely he took up our pain and bore our suffering, yet we considered him punished by God, stricken by him, and afflicted. But he was pierced for our transgressions, he was crushed for our iniquities; the punishment that brought us peace was on him, and by his wounds we are healed. *(Isaiah 53:4-5, NIV)*

Who Himself bore our sins in His own body on the tree, that we, having died to sins, might live for righteousness—by whose stripes you were healed. *(1 Peter 2:24, NKJV)*

This fulfilled the word of the Lord through the prophet Isaiah, who said, "He took our sicknesses and removed our diseases." *(Matthew 8:17, NLT)*

Search me, God, and know my heart; test me and know my anxious thoughts. *(Psalm 139:23, NIV)*

And be kind to one another, tenderhearted, forgiving one another, even as God in Christ forgave you. *(Ephesians 4:32, NKJV)*

A heart at peace gives life to the body. *(Proverbs 14:30a, NIV)*

But for you who fear my name, the Sun of Righteousness will rise with healing in his wings. And you will go free, leaping with joy like calves let out to pasture. *(Malachi 4:2, NLT)*

But you shall serve the LORD your God, and He will bless your bread and your water; and I will remove sickness from your midst. There shall be no one miscarrying or barren in your land; I will fulfill the number of your days. *(Exodus 23:25-26, NASB)*

Bless the LORD, O my soul,
And forget not all His benefits:
Who forgives all your iniquities,
Who heals all your diseases,
Who redeems your life from destruction,
Who crowns you with lovingkindness and tender
mercies. *(Psalm 103:2-4, NKJV)*

God Restores My Joy/Happiness

Personal Prayer:

Dear Heavenly Father,

You came that I may have and enjoy life, and have it in abundance (to the full, till it overflows). It is Your will that the righteous be glad and rejoice before You and that I may be happy and joyful. When I am worried, sad or anxious, comfort me and make me happy again for the joy of the Lord is my strength. Even though weeping may endure for a night, joy comes in the morning. Because my hope is in Christ, I am filled with a joy that cannot be explained, a joy full of glory. Thank you for restoring my joy. Help me to always be joyful, always keep praying, and no matter what happens, always be thankful.

Scriptures to Meditate On:

The thief comes only in order to steal and kill and destroy. I came that they may have and enjoy life, and have it in abundance (to the full, till it overflows). *(John 10:10, AMP)*

But may the righteous be glad and rejoice before God; may they be happy and joyful. *(Psalm 68:3, NIV)*

I was very worried, but you comforted me and made me happy. *(Psalm: 94:19, NCV)*

Do not grieve, for the joy of the LORD is your strength. *(Nehemiah 8:10b, NIV)*

For His anger is but for a moment, His favor is for life; Weeping may endure for a night, but joy comes in the morning. *(Psalm 30:5, NKJV)*

Happy are those who are strong in the Lord, who want above all else to follow your steps. *(Psalm, 84:5, TLB)*

A joyful heart is good medicine, but depression drains one's strength. *(Proverbs 17:22, GW)*

You have not seen Christ, but still you love him. You cannot see him now, but you believe in him. So you are filled with a joy that cannot be explained, a joy full of glory. *(1 Peter 1:8, NCV)*

Always be joyful. Always keep on praying. No matter what happens, always be thankful, for this is God's will for you who belong to Christ Jesus.
(1 Thessalonians 5:16-18, TLB)

Recommended Resource:

Giving Thanks-Why It Makes You Happy, Fills You With Peace and Changes Your Life! *by Krystal Kuehn*

18

God Restores My Confidence

Personal Prayer:

Dear Heavenly Father,

Help me to be confident, strong and courageous and not be afraid or discouraged, for You will be with me wherever I go. You are on my side. You have not given me a spirit of fear, but of power and of love and of a sound mind. For I can do everything that You ask me to do with the help of Christ who gives me the strength and power. You are my confidence. The righteous are bold as a lion. Because of Christ, I can come boldly and confidently into Your presence. Thank You Lord and all glory to You, who is able, through Your mighty power at work within me, to accomplish infinitely more in my life than I might ask, think or imagine.

Scriptures to Meditate On:

Have I not commanded you? Be strong and courageous. Do not be afraid; do not be discouraged, for the LORD your God will be with you wherever you go. *(Joshua 1:9, NIV)*

For the LORD will be at your side and will keep your foot from being snared. *(Proverbs 3:26, NIV)*

For the LORD will be your confidence, and will keep your foot from being caught. *(Proverbs 3:26, NKJV)*

For God has not given us a spirit of fear, but of power and of love and of a sound mind. *(2 Timothy 1:7, NKJV)*

For I can do everything God asks me to with the help of Christ who gives me the strength and power. *(Philippians 4:13, TLB)*

The wicked flee when no one pursues, but the righteous are bold as a lion. *(Proverbs 28:1, NKJV)*

Because of Christ and our faith in him, we can now come boldly and confidently into God's presence. *(Ephesians 3:12, NLT)*

Now all glory to God, who is able, through his mighty power at work within us, to accomplish infinitely more than we might ask or think. *(Ephesians 3:20, NLT)*

Recommended Resources:

In Christ, I Am: God's Promises on Who You Are in Christ that Will Transform You from the Inside Out *by Krystal Kuehn & Violet James*

Think Like a Winner *by Krystal Kuehn*

God Restores My Faith

Personal Prayer:

Dear Heavenly Father,

When doubts fill my mind, Your comfort gives me renewed hope and cheer. If I can believe and have faith in God, all things are possible. Nothing is impossible with You. Lord, help me to believe. Help my unbelief! Help me to walk by faith and not by sight for faith comes by hearing, and hearing by the word of God. I will meditate on Your Word day and night. I will stop doubting and believe. I will be on guard, courageous and strong standing firm in the faith; taking up my shield of faith that will extinguish all the flaming arrows of the evil one. Lord, thank you for renewed faith and that I may someday say that I have fought the good fight, I have finished the race, and I have kept the faith.

Scriptures to Meditate On:

When doubts filled my mind, your comfort gave me renewed hope and cheer. *(Psalm 94:19, NLT)*

So He asked his father, "How long has this been happening to him?" And he said, "From childhood. And often he has thrown him both into the fire and into the water to destroy him. But if You can do anything, have compassion on us and help us." Jesus said to him, "If you can believe, all things are possible to him who believes." Immediately the father of the child cried out and said with tears, "Lord, I believe; help my unbelief!" *(Mark 9:21-24, NKJV)*

"Have faith in God," Jesus answered. *(Mark 11:22, NIV)*

He replied, "Because you have so little faith. Truly I tell you, if you have faith as small as a mustard seed, you can say to this mountain, 'Move from here to there,' and it will move. Nothing will be impossible for you." *(Matthew 17:20, NIV)*

For we walk by faith, not by sight. *(2 Corinthians 5:7, NKJV)*

Now faith is confidence in what we hope for and assurance about what we do not see. *(Hebrews 11:1, NIV)*

So then faith comes by hearing, and hearing by the word of God. *(Romans 10:17, NKJV)*

Be on your guard; stand firm in the faith; be courageous; be strong. *(1 Corinthians 16:13, NIV)*

In addition to all this, take up the shield of faith, with which you can extinguish all the flaming arrows of the evil one. *(Ephesians 6:16, NIV)*

I have fought the good fight, I have finished the race, I have kept the faith. *(2 Timothy 4:7, NIV)*

"Truly I tell you, if anyone says to this mountain, 'Go, throw yourself into the sea,' and does not doubt in their heart but believes that what they say will happen, it will be done for them. Therefore I tell you, whatever you ask for in prayer, believe that you have received it, and it will be yours." *(Mark 11:23-24, NIV)*

For in Christ Jesus neither circumcision nor uncircumcision has any value. The only thing that counts is faith expressing itself through love. *(Galatians 5:6, NIV)*

Recommended Resources:

Knowing God Personally *by Krystal Kuehn*

The 10 Biggest Lies About God and the Truth That Will Set You Free *by Krystal Kuehn*

God Restores My Self-Worth

Personal Prayer:

Dear Heavenly Father,

When I feel unworthy and as if nothing I do is good enough, show me the wonders of Your great love towards me. Your word says that neither death nor life, nor angels nor principalities nor powers, nor things present nor things to come, nor height nor depth, nor any other created thing, shall be able to separate me from Your love. You keep me as the apple of Your eye for I am fearfully and wonderfully made. Your works are wonderful. I am chosen and special and made in Your image and likeness. I am a child of the most high God. Even the very hairs of my head are numbered for I am of such value in Your sight. Thank You for unconditionally loving me just as I am. May I walk worthy of the Lord, fully pleasing You, being fruitful in every good work and increasing in the knowledge of You.

Scriptures to Meditate On:

Show me the wonders of your great love, you who save by your right hand those who take refuge in you from their foes. Keep me as the apple of your eye; hide me in the shadow of your wings. *(Psalm 17:7-8, NIV)*

For I am persuaded that neither death nor life, nor angels nor principalities nor powers, nor things present nor things to come, nor height nor depth, nor any other created thing, shall be able to separate us from the love of God which is in Christ Jesus our Lord. *(Romans 8:38-39, NKJV)*

For you created my inmost being; you knit me together in my mother's womb. I praise you because I am fearfully and wonderfully made; your works are wonderful, I know that full well. *(Psalm 139: 13-14, NIV)*

Then God said, "Let us make mankind in our image, in our likeness, so that they may rule over the fish in the sea and the birds in the sky, over the livestock and all the wild animals, and over all the creatures that move along the ground." *(Genesis 1:26, NIV)*

But you are a chosen generation, a royal priesthood, a holy nation, His own special people, that you may proclaim the praises of Him who called you out of darkness into His marvelous light. *(1 Peter 2:9, NKJV)*

So in Christ Jesus you are all children of God through faith, for all of you who were baptized into Christ have clothed yourselves with Christ. There is neither Jew nor Gentile, neither slave nor free, nor is there male and female, for you are all one in Christ Jesus. If you belong to Christ, then you are Abraham's seed, and heirs according to the promise. *(Galatians 3:26-29, NIV)*

And because we are his children, God has sent the Spirit of his Son into our hearts, prompting us to call out, "Abba, Father." Now you are no longer a slave but God's own child. And since you are his child, God has made you his heir. *(Galatians 4:6-7, NLT)*

But the very hairs of your head are all numbered. Do not fear therefore; you are of more value than many sparrows. *(Matthew 10: 30-31, NKJV)*

His son said to him, 'Father, I have sinned against both heaven and you, and I am no longer worthy of being called your son.' "But his father said to the servants, 'Quick! Bring the finest robe in the house and put it on him. Get a ring for his finger and sandals for his feet. And kill the calf we have been fattening. We must celebrate with a feast, for this son of mine was dead and has now returned to life. He was lost, but now he is found.' So the party began. *(Luke 15: 21-24, NLT)*

We love Him because He first loved us. *(1 John 4:19, NKJV)*

For this reason we also, since the day we heard it, do not cease to pray for you, and to ask that you may be filled with the knowledge of His will in all wisdom and spiritual understanding; that you may walk worthy of the Lord, fully pleasing Him, being fruitful in every good work and increasing in the knowledge of God. *(Colossians 1:9-10, NKJV)*

Recommended Resource:

In Christ, I Am: God's Promises on Who You Are in Christ that Will Transform You from the Inside Out *by Krystal Kuehn & Violet James*

God Restores My Time and Opportunities

Personal Prayer:

Dear Heavenly Father,

Teach me to number my days that I may gain a heart of wisdom. I realize the brevity of life; it is but a breath, a vapor. I have made some wrong decisions and I have not made the most of every opportunity. If I could go back in time, I would do things differently. Help me, today, to walk in wisdom so that I may redeem and make the best use of my time and new opportunities. I know that when one door closes, another door opens. Guide me in the direct path for my life and give me the wisdom, strength and courage to pursue it. I want to make the hours of my life more fruitful and the years of my life more productive. I want my life to honor and please You, and to produce every kind of good fruit. You are the vine, I am the branch. Help me to remain in You, so that I may produce much fruit. Thank you for redeeming my time and opening new and better opportunities in my life.

Scriptures to Meditate On:

Teach us to number our days that we may gain a heart of wisdom. *(Psalm 90:12, NIV)*

You have given me only a short life; my lifetime is like nothing to you. Everyone's life is only a breath. *(Psalm 39L5, NCV)*

There is a **time for everything**, and a season for every activity under the heavens:

a time to be born and a time to die,
a time to plant and a time to uproot,
 a time to kill and a time to heal,
a time to tear down and a time to build,
a time to weep and a time to laugh,
a time to mourn and a time to dance,
a time to scatter stones and a time to gather them,
a time to embrace and a time to refrain from embracing,
a time to search and a time to give up,
a time to keep and a time to throw away,
a time to tear and a time to mend,
a time to be silent and a time to speak,
a time to love and a time to hate,
a time for war and a time for peace.
(Ecclesiastes 3:1-8, NIV)

See then that you walk circumspectly, not as fools but as wise, redeeming the time, because the days are evil. *(Ephesians 5:15-16, NKJV)*

Write this to the angel of the church in Philadelphia: "This is what the One who is holy and true, who holds the key of David, says. When he opens a door, no one can close it. And when he closes it, no one can open it." *(Revelation 3:7, NCV)*

I, Wisdom, will make the hours of your day more profitable and the years of your life more fruitful. *(Proverbs 9:11, TLB)*

Seek his will in all you do, and he will show you which path to take. *(Proverbs 3:6, NLT)*

So we have not stopped praying for you since we first heard about you. We ask God to give you complete knowledge of his will and to give you spiritual wisdom and understanding. Then the way you live will always honor and please the Lord, and your lives will produce every kind of good fruit. All the while, you will grow as you learn to know God better and better. *(Colossians 1:9-10, NLT)*

"Yes, I am the vine; you are the branches. Those who remain in me, and I in them, will produce much fruit. For apart from me you can do nothing." *(John 15:5, NLT)*

Recommended Resource:

21 Power Habits for a Winning Life with Empowering Affirmations & Words of Wisdom *(Volumes One and Two)* by Krystal Kuehn

God Restores My Freedom

Personal Prayer:

Dear Heavenly Father,

I pray that You help me to walk in freedom from
_____ (bondage to sin, destructive habits,
addiction). Jesus purchased my freedom with His
blood and forgave my sins. Sin is no longer my
master. And, I am no longer a captive but I am set
free. I live under the freedom of God's grace. I will
walk in freedom, for I have devoted myself to your
Word and promises. I shall know the truth, and the
truth shall make me free. There is freedom in Christ.
Where the Spirit of the Lord is there is liberty. I no
longer have to struggle with sin, for I have been called
to live in freedom. Thank you, Lord that I am free
and I will use my freedom to serve one another in
love.

Scriptures to Meditate On:

He is so rich in kindness and grace that he purchased
our freedom with the blood of his Son and forgave our
sins. *(Ephesians 1:7, NLT)*

Sin is no longer your master, for you no longer live
under the requirements of the law. Instead, you live

under the freedom of God's grace. *(Romans 6:14, NLT)*

I will walk in freedom, for I have devoted myself to your commandments. *(Psalm 119:45, NLT)*

Now the Lord is the Spirit; and where the Spirit of the Lord is, there is liberty. *(2 Corinthians 3:17, NKJV)*

And you shall know the truth, and the truth shall make you free. *(John 8:32, NKJV)*

But God is so rich in mercy, and he loved us so much, that even though we were dead because of our sins, he gave us life when he raised Christ from the dead. (It is only by God's grace that you have been saved!) For he raised us from the dead along with Christ and seated us with him in the heavenly realms because we are united with Christ Jesus. *(Ephesians 2:4-6, NLT)*

But the Scriptures declare that we are all prisoners of sin, so we receive God's promise of freedom only by believing in Jesus Christ. *(Galatians 3:22, NLT)*

For you have been called to live in freedom, my brothers and sisters. But don't use your freedom to satisfy your sinful nature. Instead, use your freedom to serve one another in love. *(Galatians 5:13, NLT)*

The Lord GOD has put his Spirit in me, because the LORD has appointed me to tell the good news to the poor. He has sent me to comfort those whose hearts are broken, to tell the captives they are free, and to tell the prisoners they are released. *(Isaiah 61:1, NCV)*

It is for freedom that Christ has set us free. Stand firm, then, and do not let yourselves be burdened again by a yoke of slavery. *(Galatians 5:1, NIV)*

God Restores My Relationships

Personal Prayer:

Dear Heavenly Father,

I pray that you help restore my relationship with
_____ (friend, spouse, family member, child,
partner, worker). Help me to be willing to let go of
offenses and grudges that I am holding on to because I
feel wronged and hurt. Help me to be a peacemaker -
understanding, kind, merciful, patient, and loving for
love never fails. I will not blame others but take
responsibility for my part and mistakes. I ask that
You please forgive me for my wrong words, attitudes
and actions in this relationship. Help me to be careful
what I say, a good listener, slow to speak and slow to
get angry. Thank You, Lord, for restoring and healing
the wounds in this relationship. May we have a loving
and healthy relationship once again.

Scriptures to Meditate On:

Blessed are the peacemakers, for they will be called
children of God. *(Matthew 5:9, NIV)*

And those who are peacemakers will plant seeds of
peace and reap a harvest of righteousness. *(James
3:18, NLT)*

Love is patient, love is kind. It does not envy, it does not boast, it is not proud. It does not dishonor others, it is not self-seeking, it is not easily angered, it keeps no record of wrongs. Love does not delight in evil but rejoices with the truth. It always protects, always trusts, always hopes, always perseveres.

Love never fails. But where there are prophecies, they will cease; where there are tongues, they will be stilled; where there is knowledge, it will pass away. *(1 Corinthians 13:4-8, NIV)*

Since God chose you to be the holy people he loves, you must clothe yourselves with tenderhearted mercy, kindness, humility, gentleness, and patience. *(Colossians 3:12, NLT)*

My dear brothers and sisters, take note of this: Everyone should be quick to listen, slow to speak and slow to become angry. *(James 1:19, NIV)*

Get rid of all bitterness, rage, anger, harsh words, and slander, as well as all types of evil behavior. *(Ephesians 4:31, NLT)*

Be kindly affectionate to one another with brotherly love, in honor giving preference to one another. *(Romans 12:10, NKLV)*

The Lord's Prayer:

Our Father in heaven, may your name be kept holy.
May your Kingdom come soon.
May your will be done on earth, as it is in heaven.
Give us today the food we need,
and forgive us our sins, as we have forgiven those
who sin against us.
And don't let us yield to temptation, but rescue us
from the evil one. *(Matthew 6:9-13, NLT)*

Recommended Resources:

10 Keys to Happy & Loving Relationships *by
Krystal Kuehn*

Restore Your Marriage & Fall in Love Again *by
Krystal Kuehn*

God Restores My Trust/ Heart from Betrayal

Personal Prayer:

Dear Heavenly Father,

When people (family, friends, workers, etc.) fail and betray me, restore and heal my heart from the hurt and pain. My trust is lost. Jesus knows what it feels like to be betrayed by someone close. He experienced deep hurt and betrayal as well. So, You understand my deep pain and anguish. I am crying out to You and You promise that those who trust in You will not be put to shame. Thank you that Your mercy and unfailing love surround and comfort me. For You keep me in perfect peace when my mind is stayed on You. Help me to restore my faith and trust in others, myself and in You. Thank You that You are my shield and that You defend and comfort me.

Scriptures to Meditate On:

To you they cried out and were saved; in you they trusted and were not put to shame. *(Psalm 22:5, NIV)*

Many are the woes of the wicked, but the Lord's unfailing love surrounds the one who trusts in him. *(Psalm 32:10, NIV)*

[Jesus Predicts His Betrayal] "I am not referring to all of you; I know those I have chosen. But this is to fulfill this passage of Scripture: 'He who shared my bread has turned against me." *(John 13:18, NIV)*

[Betrayal and Arrest in Gethsemane] And while He was still speaking, behold, a multitude; and he who was called Judas, one of the twelve, went before them and drew near to Jesus to kiss Him. *(Luke 22:47, NKJV)*

You will keep him in perfect peace, whose mind is stayed on You, because he trusts in You. *(Isaiah 26:3, NKJV)*

Even my close friend,
    someone I trusted,
one who shared my bread,
    has turned against me.
But may you have mercy on me, LORD;
    raise me up, that I may repay them.
I know that you are pleased with me,
    for my enemy does not triumph over me.
Because of my integrity you uphold me
    and set me in your presence forever.
(Psalm 41:9-13, NIV)

As for God, His way is perfect;
The word of the LORD is proven;
He is a shield to all who trust in Him.
(2 Samuel 22:31, NKJV)

God Restores My Child

Personal Prayer:

Dear Heavenly Father,

I trust and release my child (_____) to You. You have good plans and a purpose for his/her life. You have plans to prosper (_____) and to give him/her hope and a future. My child will not be doomed to misfortune but delivered from evil. And because You are my shelter and refuge, my child is blessed, protected and prosperous and no evil will conquer him/her and no curse will come near my home. No weapon formed against (_____) will prosper. I ask that You help me to be the parent You want me to be. Give me wisdom, discernment and guidance when dealing with (_____). Help my child know that he/she is loved and accepted. Remove people that are a bad influence on him/her and replace them with godly friends and role models. I pray that my child will hunger and thirst after righteousness and know You personally. I thank You that (_____) is a gift from You and that he/she will fulfill what You have called him/her to do. Thank You, Lord for restoring, protecting, guiding and watching over my child.

Scriptures to Meditate On:

"For I know the plans I have for you," declares the Lord, "plans to prosper you and not to harm you, plans to give you hope and a future." *(Jeremiah 29:11, NIV)*

The righteous man walks in his integrity; His children are blessed after him. *(Proverbs 20:7, NKJV)*

If you make the LORD your refuge, if you make the Most High your shelter, no evil will conquer you; no plague will come near your home. *(Psalm 91:9-10, NLT)*

They will not work in vain, and their children will not be doomed to misfortune. For they are people blessed by the LORD, and their children, too, will be blessed. *(Isaiah 65:23, NLT)*

"No weapon formed against you shall prosper, And every tongue which rises against you in judgment You shall condemn. This is the heritage of the servants of the LORD, And their righteousness is from Me," Says the LORD. *(Isaiah 54:17, NKJV)*

If any of you lacks wisdom, let him ask of God, who gives to all liberally and without reproach, and it will be given to him. *(James 1:5, NKJV)*

Children are a gift from the LORD; they are a reward from him. *(Psalm 127:3, NLT)*

The righteous man walks in his integrity; His children are blessed after him. *(Proverbs 20:7, NKJV)*

44

Blessed are those who hunger and thirst for righteousness, for they will be filled. *(Matthew 5:6, NIV)*

God **Restores My Finances**

Personal Prayer:

Dear Heavenly Father,

You are Jehovah-Jireh, my provider. You supply all my needs according to Your riches in glory by Christ Jesus. Abraham's blessing is mine. Financial blessing and abundant provision are Your will for my life. Therefore, I will not suffer from want or lack anything. I will not be afraid, troubled or anxious about my finances. You are the unfailing, unlimited source of my supply. I pray all my debts are paid off and bills paid on time. My financial income now increases as Your blessings overtake me. Give me wisdom and understanding and lead me to make wise and prosperous financial decisions. Guide me in all truth regarding my financial affairs. Whatever I do succeeds and prospers because my steps are directed by You. I am like a tree planted by rivers of water. I bring forth fruit in my season, my leaf will not wither, and whatever I do will prosper. As I give, it is given unto me, good measure, pressed down, shaken together, and running over. Thank You that I have more than enough to not only meet all of my needs but that I can also be a blessing to others.

Scriptures to Meditate On:

And Abraham called the name of that place Jehovah-Jireh: as it is said to this day, In the mount of the LORD it shall be seen. *(Genesis 22:14, KJV)*

And my God shall supply all your need according to His riches in glory by Christ Jesus. *(Philippians 4:19, NKJV)*

Beloved, I pray that you may prosper in all things and be in health, just as your soul prospers. *(3 John 1:2, NKJV)*

Peace I leave with you, My peace I give to you; not as the world gives do I give to you. Let not your heart be troubled, neither let it be afraid. *(John 14:27, NKJV)*

Give, and it will be given to you. A good measure, pressed down, shaken together and running over, will be poured into your lap. For with the measure you use, it will be measured to you. *(Luke 6:38, NIV)*

..that the blessing of Abraham might come upon the Gentiles in Christ Jesus, that we might receive the promise of the Spirit through faith. *(Galatians 3:14, NKJV)*

A man's heart plans his way, but the LORD directs his steps. *(Proverbs 16:9, NKJV)*

Blessed is the one
   who does not walk in step with the wicked
or stand in the way that sinners take
   or sit in the company of mockers,
but whose delight is in the law of the LORD,
   and who meditates on his law day and night.
That person is like a tree planted by streams of water,
   which yields its fruit in season
and whose leaf does not wither—
   whatever they do prospers. *(Psalm 1: 1-3, NIV)*

You may say to yourself, "My power and the strength of my hands have produced this wealth for me." But remember the LORD your God, for it is he who gives you the ability to produce wealth, and so confirms his covenant, which he swore to your ancestors, as it is today. *(Deuteronomy 8:17-18, NIV)*

And all these blessings shall come upon you and overtake you, because you obey the voice of the LORD your God. *(Deuteronomy 28:2, NKJV)*

Let them shout for joy and be glad,
Who favor my righteous cause;
And let them say continually,
"Let the LORD be magnified,
Who has pleasure in the prosperity of His servant."
(Psalm 35:27, NKJV)

Recommended Resource:

5 Simple Steps to Get Out of Debt: Live Debt-Free
& Experience Financial Freedom *by Violet James*

Are You in Christ and is Christ in You?

Jesus Christ has made the Father God known to us: "I have made You known to them, and will continue to make You known in order that the love You have for Me may be in them and that I Myself may be in them" (John 17:26, NIV). God wants us to receive His love. In doing so, we will be in Christ and He will be in us.

First, it must be understood that God's love is freely given to us in His Son and His love holds no conditions. There is nothing you can do to EARN God's love. It doesn't matter how many times or how hard you try to be a good person or live a worthy live. "For by GRACE you have been saved through FAITH, and that not of yourselves; it is the GIFT OF GOD, not of works, lest anyone should boast" (Eph. 2:8, 9; emphasis added). Salvation is a gift of God. It is not our reward for doing good things on earth.

Secondly, we must recognize that we "all fall short of God's glorious ideal" (Romans 3:23, TLB). We ALL have sinned and there is punishment for sin. God doesn't want us to face the eternal judgment for sin and that is why He sent His Son to die in our place. Jesus Christ paid the price for our sins and He redeemed us with His precious blood (1 Peter 1:18,

19). In order to be saved, we must acknowledge our sin and repent.

The Bible says that you can choose to be in Christ. You can choose to go from eternal death (separation from God) to eternal life. "If you **confess with your mouth** the Lord Jesus and **believe in your heart** that God raised Him from the dead, you will be saved. For with the heart one believes unto righteousness and with the mouth confession is made unto salvation (Romans 10:9, 10).

If you want to know that you are in Christ and that He is in you, pray this prayer to God:

Dear Heavenly Father,

I thank you for sending Jesus to die for my sins so that I may have eternal life and a personal relationship with You. I confess that I am a sinner and come short of Your glory. I repent and ask for your forgiveness. I understand that it is by grace that I am saved through faith, and there is nothing I can do to earn salvation. I believe in my heart that Jesus Christ is the Son of God. I believe He was raised from the dead for my justification. And I confess Him now as my Lord and Savior. The blood of Jesus Christ has cleansed me from all sin and now I am a child of God and I am saved. Thank You, Father. In Jesus' name, amen.

About the Author

Violet James, MSM is a best-selling author, an entrepreneur, marketing and business manager, award-winning web designer, and artist. For over 20 years she has been sharing and ministering God's love, hope and healing through her books, ministries and outreaches.

She is the cofounder and executive director of Christian-Kindle-Books.com, NewDayCounseling.org and NewDayMusicOutreach.com.

Connect with Violet James

It is my sincerest desire and hope God Restores: Prayers and Promises for Restoration has helped you to discover that God will comfort you, heal your pain and sorrow, strengthen you and restore every area of your life. I would love to hear your testimonials and how you have been helped. You can send your testimonials, feedback and comments to me at:

maxpotential312@gmail.com

I encourage you to share your experience, and I would truly appreciate if you would **write a review** on Amazon.

My author profile:
http://www.amazon.com/author/violetjames

Join the Words of Inspiration page
and Friend us on Facebook:
http://www.facebook.com/WordsOfInspiration

Follow and connect with us on Twitter:
http://www.twitter.com/behappy4lifeNDC

Visit the Be Your Best blog (offers RSS):
http://www.newdaycounselingcenter.blogspot.com/

LinkedIn: http://www.linkedin.com/in/violetjames

Books by Violet James & Krystal Kuehn (sister):

In Christ, I am... God's Promises on Who You Are in Christ that Will Transform You from the Inside Out

God's Promises in 8 Keys Life Areas That Will Change Your Life

Your Free Gift

As a way of saying *thanks* for your purchase, we're offering this free must-have book that's exclusive to our readers.

7 Things to Do Every Day for a Prosperous Day
by Krystal Kuehn, MA, LPC, LLP, NCC

Live each new day with victory and joy!!

When you subscribe to our newsletter via email, you will get free, immediate access to download the ebook.

You can download this free ebook by going here:

http://www.christian-kindle-books.com/FreeGift.html

36107691R00042

Made in the USA
Lexington, KY
07 October 2014